Classroom Management

Non-Compliance

Four Strategies That Work

Ennio Cipani

CARL A. RUDISILL LIBRARY
LENOIR-RHYNE COLLEGE

Published by The Council for Exceptional Children

Library of Congress Cataloging-in-Publication Data

Cipani, Ennio.
   Non-compliance : four strategies that work / Ennio Cipani.
     p. cm.
   "CEC mini-library: classroom management."
   Includes bibliographical references.
   ISBN 0-86586-238-9
   1. Behavior modification. 2. Compliance. 3. Classroom management. I. Title.
LB1060.2.C57 1993
371.5—dc20   93-26753
                                                                                                                                  CIP

ISBN 0-86586-238-9

Copyright 1993 by The Council for Exceptional Children, 1920 Association Drive, Reston, Virginia 22091-1589

Stock No. P389

All rights reserved. No part of this publication may be reproduced, stored in a retrieval system, or transmitted, in any form or by any means, electronic, mechanical, photocopying, recording, or otherwise, without the prior written permission of the copyright owner.

Printed in the United States of American

10 9 8 7 6 5 4 3 2 1

Foreword

At the 1993 Annual Convention in San Antonio, Texas, The Council for Exceptional Children passed a policy on physical intervention that stresses the right of each child receiving special education services to have a learning environment in which the educational strategies used are (a) the most effective for changing behavior and (b) the least restrictive possible in terms of preserving the child's dignity and personal privacy. This publication on managing non-compliance presents several alternatives to more restrictive methods of discipline. Research has shown that the strategies presented are effective and have been used successfully by professionals and parents to develop more positive behaviors in children.

Dr. Ennio Cipani has initiated this mini-library series on Classroom Management because he recognized the need to gather these techniques into an integrated collection for use by teachers and others responsible for managing problem behaviors. The books use familiar classroom scenarios for presenting each strategy. The easy-to-read style and step-by-step analysis of each strategy make the books in this series easy and fun to use.

Being a teacher of children with special needs is a rewarding albeit demanding career. The Council for Exceptional Children recognizes its responsibility to share best practices and support those who work with special children. To this end, we are pleased to add this book to our growing collection of resources.

George E. Ayers
Executive Director

August 20, 1993

Contents

Introduction 1

Purpose of This Classroom Management Manual 1

Description of Non-Compliance 2

Possible By-Products of Child Non-Compliance 3

When Is Non-Compliance a Problem? 4

How to Define Non-Compliance 5

How to Measure Non-Compliance 6

Four Techniques for Dealing with Children Who Are Non-Compliant 7

Teacher Praise and Attention 7

Guided Practice and Reinforcement 11

Grandma's Rule 15

Behavioral Momentum 20

Conclusion 23

References 24

CEC Policy on Physical Intervention 25

Introduction

Purpose of This Classroom Management Manual

The purpose of this manual is to provide teachers and other instructional personnel with an understanding of child non-compliance and techniques for dealing effectively with children who are non-compliant in the classroom. The manual describes four techniques that have been developed and validated in the applied behavior management research, in both general and special education settings. These techniques can be used in a variety of settings where children are non-compliant—in regular classes and resource programs providing consultation to regular education teachers, as well as in resource pull-out programs and special education classes and sites. To facilitate the use of these techniques with children with special needs in mainstream sites, a brochure briefly describing each of the four techniques is available from the author for your use during consultations with other instructional personnel. These brochures can also be handy resources for parents seeking more information on strategies that deal with non-compliant behavior.

This manual is particularly appropriate for instructional personnel who work with children in preschool and the elementary grades. The techniques can be employed in classrooms with older students; however,

---

The author expresses his sincere appreciation to Cindy First and Lori Tirapelle for their suggestions on the content, form, and style of this manual.

Order brochures from: Dr. Ennio Cipani, The California School of Professional Psychology, Clinical Child Psychology Program, 1350 M Street, Fresno, CA 93721.

some variation in the rewards and procedures would have to be developed. It is better for non-compliance to be addressed early in a child's educational life so that the child will receive the full benefit of classroom instruction.

Description of Non-Compliance

Ismael has to be told many times by the recess supervisor to come in from recess. Every day the same scenario plays out between them. The supervisor blows the whistle, signaling the end of the recess period. Ismael continues playing. The supervisor calls him by name, reminding him of his responsibility to line up like the other children. If this does not work, which is often the case, the supervisor must go and get him, at which point he will run away. He often spends time in the principal's office after each recess.

Julia occasionally refuses to get her pencil out of her backpack. The teacher feels that the only way to get Julia to get her pencil is to be stern with her, but lately this only seems to result in Julia's crying. The school psychologist has been contacted to see whether Julia suffers from emotional problems.

Sound familiar? Many teachers who have been in the teaching profession for some period of time have encountered such cases. We call these behavioral incidents *non-compliant behaviors,* or the failure to comply with a teacher request or instruction. While these examples may be extreme, you probably have encountered non-compliance on a more subtle level. Have you ever asked a child in your class to copy mathematics problems off the blackboard or read pages in a reading workbook, only to discover after several minutes that the child has not started the task? These are more subtle examples of non-compliance.

Non-compliance can involve a number of different behaviors, ranging from doing nothing to verbally and/or physically refusing to comply with a teacher request or instruction. The following are examples of other possible instructions or requests, along with possible non-compliant behaviors in response to those requests (child behaviors are in parentheses):

- "Recess is over, Amelia, please put away your toys!" (Amelia continues to play with toys.)

- "Please write your name and date in the upper right hand corner of your paper!" (Child puts name in lower right hand corner.)
- "Johnny, please get a pencil and a piece of paper!" (Johnny whines and cries that he doesn't want to do any work.)
- "Class, it is time to come inside from recess!" (Some children stay outside.)
- "I would appreciate it if everyone would walk in a straight line!" (Children run instead of walk.)
- "Sarah, please read quietly!" (Sarah continues to read out loud.)

Many teachers know all too well that getting a child to follow an instruction is only half the ballgame. Getting children to *refrain from* doing something is another source of concern. In this case, the teacher requests the child not to perform a specific behavior, for example, "Remember the rule! When we are in line, we do not hit each other while we are walking to the cafeteria!" "Stop throwing your pencil in class!" "Class, please do not go near the softball game during recess!" Children demonstrate non-compliant behavior when they do not heed the instruction and engage in the behavior or activity anyway.

Possible By-Products of Child Non-Compliance

Non-compliance in children can be problematic, particularly because it is often the precursor to other inappropriate and/or disruptive classroom behavior. Do you have some children who are verbally and/or physically aggressive to you or other teaching personnel? Frequent non-compliance in some young children can often foster these more serious behavior problems later on. With some children, their initial verbal refusal to comply with some request is followed by an even more serious behavior problem when the teacher attempts to get them to comply by being more forceful. This is better known as the infamous power struggle.

> Sarah, a kindergarten student, was told by Mrs. Ramirez not to throw sand out of the sand box. Sarah continued to throw sand out of the area (i.e., was non-compliant to Mrs. Ramirez). Mrs. Ramirez told her that if she threw sand out again, she would have to come and sit down on the bench for awhile.

Sarah looked at her and threw sand at another child near the sandbox (continued her non-compliance and became aggressive toward a peer). Mrs. Ramirez told Sarah she would have to get out of the sandbox, at which point Sarah fell to the ground and threw a tantrum for several minutes, while everyone on the playground watched.

A principal reviewing the note from the teacher on this incident would probably ask, "How did this happen?" It is important to note that it started with Sarah's not complying. Mrs. Ramirez then attempted to get compliance unsuccessfully. As Sarah escalated her behavior, Mrs. Ramirez was "forced" to become more involved in a punitive way, hence the full-blown tantrum.

You might be under the impression that there are more important discipline problems to deal with than non-compliance. While it seems reasonable to focus on the more serious behavior problems, such as throwing sand at the other child, it is apparent that non-compliance started the chain of events that, in this case, led to aggression and the tantrum. Of course, a heightened level of serious problem behaviors puts the child at risk for remaining in mainstreamed educational settings, particularly when attempts to alter the child's behavior prove ineffective. Child non-compliance should not be taken lightly. Hoping the child will "grow out of it" is not the answer. Frequent non-compliance needs to be addressed early in its development if it is to be arrested.

When Is Non-Compliance a Problem?

Non-compliance occurs in all children. Even your best-behaved student sometimes is mildly non-compliant. He or she *occasionally* may not follow your directions to read quietly. But you certainly would not consider this child to be non-compliant. So when do you consider a child's non-compliance to constitute a management problem? The following factors separate severely non-compliant children from others:

1. *Frequency.* The more frequent the occurrence of non-compliance, the greater the problem.

2. *Age of the child.* The younger the child, the less a problem occasional non-compliance is.

3. *Severity.* The more severe the form of the non-compliant behavior, the greater the problem.

How to Define Non-Compliance

Non-compliance has been defined in research studies as a variation of the following (Roberts, McMahon, Forehand, & Humphreys, 1978): "Failure to either initiate an appropriate motor/verbal response within five seconds of the termination of a comment or to inhibit an inappropriate motor/verbal response for the same five-second interval (p. 794)." These researchers distinguish clear commands from unclear commands. Unclear commands are commands in which the behavior being requested is vague or the child is not given an opportunity to comply. Table 1 lists examples of vague and clear commands.

Most teachers find that creating their own definition of non-compliance fits the specifics of their particular classrooms and circumstances. Coming up with a definition of your own that is workable for your classroom, rather than using a definition from a book, is a good idea. The following guidelines are important in defining non-compliance:

1. *Specify observable non-compliant behaviors.* Examples are failure to initiate a verbal response to an instruction and failure to complete an assigned task.

2. *Specify a time limit for the initiation of a response.* Somewhere in the range of 3 to 5 seconds is often adequate. This time limit identifies the point at which the child has demonstrated non-compliance with your request.

TABLE 1
Vague and Clear Directions

Vague	*Clear*
1. "Get busy!"	1. "Please begin writing the answers to questions one through five."
2. "Knock it off!"	2. "I need Johnny and Bobby to be quiet while I am calling the class roll."
3. "Please empty the trash!"	3. "Take care of the trash in the dumpster outside, and return in time to begin the math assignment (in 2 minutes).

3. *Specify a time limit for completing the designated activity.* This time limit specifies the length of time the child has to perform the task assigned. The time limit can vary as a function of the request being made. For example, a request to name the three states that border California might specify a time limit of 8 to 10 seconds for completing the verbal response. However, cleaning the chalkboard might require a 5-minute time limit for completion.

How to Measure Non-Compliance

Non-compliance is usually measured by recording the frequency at which it occurs—that is, simply counting the number of times a child does not follow instructions. An example would be the number of times Susan failed to bring in her homework. A better way to determine the level of a child's non-compliance is to get the percentage of times the child complies out of the total number of requests or instructions given. An example would be the percentage of times Johnny did not get in line for lunch. Of course, when measuring percentage of occurrence, the teacher must keep track of the total number of times instructions or requests were presented. For example, if Johnny was in line (within a designated period of time) 15 times in a 1-week period and was not in the line 5 times, his percentage of not getting in line for that week is 25%. To help in the data collection effort, here is a list of tips.

Tips for Gathering Data

1. Use wrist counters whenever possible.
2. Have a data sheet readily available to you to record frequency of occurrence.
3. Use a tape recorder whenever possible to record entries of behavior, as well as recording the child's name. This is a good way to collect data on many children.
4. Realize that you have other duties. Sometimes just collecting data once or twice every 2 to 3 weeks may have to suffice.

Four Techniques for Dealing with Children Who Are Non-Compliant

There is no one way to deal with all non-compliant children. Not one of the four techniques offered here will work for every child. The selection of which technique to implement for a particular child should be guided by information gathered about the particular child and the possible reason(s) for the non-compliance.

Teacher Praise and Attention

"He did that for my attention!" "She doesn't listen because her friends think it's cute!" Sometimes non-compliance is the result of the attention it receives, whether you consider the form of the attention to be reminders or negative or positive comments. "Catch them being good" is the slogan for cases of non-compliance that are a result of teacher attention to the (mis)behavior. "Catch them being good" involves praising children when they do comply, while withholding praise and attention for acts of non-compliance. The following example describes a case of a child who apparently refuses to comply with the teacher's request to get in line simply to gain the teacher's attention.

> The teacher observes repeatedly that whenever Johnny is asked to get in line (to go with the class to another activity), he usually has to be told many times before he eventually lines up with his classmates. When he does not respond to repeated requests, very often the teacher must go over and ask him nicely to get in line: "John, I have asked you three

times already to get in line. It is time to go to the lunchroom. I would really like it if you got in line." He usually then lines up and seems to enjoy this personal attention. The teacher also notes that the few times he did line up upon the first or second request, the teacher forgot to praise him and went about calling others to the line. The teacher rationalizes this mistake by saying that it was such a shock to see Johnny get in line that it left her speechless! Nevertheless, Johnny sees that in order to get special attention he must act as if he did not hear the teacher the first couple of times she asked him to get in line. This information lends evidence to the possibility that Johnny's non-compliance is motivated by the teacher's attention.

This scenario points up several factors to note when examining the possibility of teacher attention as the reason for a child's non-compliance. First, it is evident that some form of verbal or non-verbal teacher attention follows the non-compliance. Sometimes the child can be cajoled or coaxed into complying by the teacher (or a peer) after the initial non-compliant act. It is also apparent that teacher attention for other behaviors such as compliance is usually low. In other words, non-compliance gets more of the teacher's attention than compliance. Finally, peer attention should also be considered as a possible motivator for a child's non-compliance.

Teacher Praise and Attention Techniques

The following steps should be followed in using praise and attention.

1. Present the instruction or request once in clear behavioral terms.
2. State the time limit for complying with the request or instruction or the time limit for initiating a response.
3. Provide contingent praise and attention if the student complies with your request or initiates a response within the time limit.
4. Withhold your praise and attention if compliance is not obtained within the time limit.
5. Provide gentle guidance after the time limit elapses to obtain compliance at that time (without praise or comment). *Note.* This may require a written behavioral program and the consent of parents and the individualized education program (IEP) team in many states.

The instruction or request should be stated in clear terms so that there is no ambiguity as to the behavior that is expected. For example, the instruction "Johnny, I want you to line up behind Susan" leaves little room for ambiguity. On the other hand, "Johnny, get with it" may be misconstrued, especially by young children. The child also needs to be told the time limit for complying with your request. When appropriate, you can indicate that you are going to count (e.g., "I'm going to count to three!") as the method of determining the length of time to be allotted, particularly if the time allotted to initiate a response is only 3 to 5 seconds. In cases when the child has to complete a task, it might be more appropriate to set a portable oven timer or a stopwatch. The instruction should then be given in this manner, "I'm setting the timer for 2 minutes. You have 2 minutes to clean off your desk of all papers and materials, put your books in your backpack, and get in line!" Note that this instruction leaves little doubt as to what is expected of the child and the length of time in which it is to be completed.

Most teachers are very good at providing praise for good work. Now consider using praise for compliance to your requests and instructions. Providing *enthusiastic*, animated praise and possibly additional tangible rewards for compliance *when it occurs* is an essential part of this strategy. Failing to praise compliance will make the overall plan for reducing non-compliance less effective. If appropriate, give hugs, handshakes, or other forms of approval. Also, if appropriate, provide points to be traded in for other primary rewards.

One comment on providing praise for compliance is in order here. Some teachers respond to the suggestion with, "I don't have the time. I have too many children to be targeting one or more children for all this praise. The rest of the children will suffer because of all the attention these few target children are receiving." If you are on the receiving end of this "venting" it is important to deal with it in a professional manner. First, *listen* to the teacher who is venting. It is possible that using such a strategy may *initially* take a lot of the teacher's time, and she or he may feel overwhelmed. *Consistently* praising appropriate behavior is a new skill for some people, and it will feel like it takes an inordinate amount of time. However, you can point out to the teacher that the skill will become easier, feel more natural, and become an inherent part of his or her teaching repertoire once it is learned. After the new skill is learned, the teacher may not have to invest any more time in dealing with compliance situations than previously. Very often, non-compliant children receive no more attention with this strategy than they were receiving prior to the teacher's praising compliant behavior. The amount of attention is just shifted from children's non-compliant acts to their acts of compliance.

You can also point out that as a child's behavior improves, the need for other aspects of the technique (e.g., gentle guidance) is reduced. The teacher will be able to engage in other activities once the child begins to comply more frequently because time previously spent on dealing with non-compliance is freed up for other things. Finally, the teacher must realize that compliance problems are not likely to go away by themselves. There is an appropriate saying you can use with teachers who do not want to entertain any other strategy: "If you keep doing what you're doing, you'll keep getting what you're getting." Sometimes you just have to go and do it!

If a student does not comply within the time allotted or does not initiate a response, do not offer attention or verbal praise. Do not make additional requests (i.e., give reminders) or plead with the child to comply at that point. This is not intended to make you the "meany of the block." It is intended to serve as a mechanism to teach the child that your attention follows only compliance with your initial request, not non-compliance. It might also be necessary to gently guide the young child to comply with the request, if feasible. This component may need a written plan submitted to the IEP team and consented to by team members and parents.

Let's see how this technique looks in practice:

> Mrs. Jones decides to implement a contingent teacher praise and attention strategy for Billy's non-compliance to her requests to get in line. She begins by stating to him very clearly, "Billy, it is your turn to line up. I will count to five Mississippi. You need to be in the line behind Jessie before I reach five Mississippi (see Steps 1 and 2, page 8)." She then proceeds to count. When he gets in line ahead of the count, she praises him *fervently* and also gives him a star that he trades in later in the day for his choice of activities and items during free play (Step 3). When he is non-compliant, she does not say another word, but merely guides him to his spot in the line (Step 5). She does not offer praise or other reinforcers during this guidance (Step 4). She then proceeds to call on the other children, or groups of children (reinforcing them for compliance with praise and points).

Additional Suggestions and Considerations

1. Initially, select just a few instructions or requests to which the child is non-compliant. If the strategy is successful with those initial

instructions, you can implement it over a wider range of instructions, tasks, settings, and other children.
2. If you are going to award points for compliance (in addition to praise and teacher attention), then draw up a chart that specifies how many points are needed to purchase rewarding items, activities, or events.
3. If peer reinforcement is the factor responsible for the student's non-compliance, then use a group reinforcement strategy (see Litow & Pumroy, 1975 for details on group reinforcement contingencies).
4. Peer reinforcement is more likely with older students (e.g., intermediate, middle school/junior high, high school) than with young children as a reason for non-compliance.
5. If peer reinforcement is responsible for non-compliance, contingent withdrawal of teacher attention is not the appropriate technique in most circumstances. Instead, strategies designed to remove peer attention for non-compliance are indicated (see item 3).
6. If this technique is successful in dealing with the non-compliance problem, continue its use. If not, try another technique.

Guided Practice and Reinforcement

You may surmise that sometimes young children, particularly, do not respond to your requests because they are unsure of the intent of the request. If non-compliance is the result of a child's inability to understand the content or meaning of the request, then guided practice and reinforcement is the management strategy of choice. Children who *lack the skill* to comply with specific requests or commands do not seek teacher attention for their non-compliance. Rather, it is often their failure to understand the command, instruction, or request that is the reason for their non-compliance. In some cases, the child may be unaware of what behavior is being requested. In other cases, it may be a limited attention span that prohibits the child from attending to and processing the entire set of instructions and, therefore, limits the child's ability to comply.

> Whenever Ramona is asked to get in line to go with the class to another activity, she either doesn't respond to these instructions or gets in the wrong line (e.g., lines up to go to the bathroom instead of lining up to go outside). Mr. Anastasi has noticed that Ramona often gets other instructions and

requests mixed up. This information lends evidence to the possibility that Ramona's non-compliance to certain requests is because she either does not understand the instruction or does not know the steps involved in complying with the instruction.

If Ramona's failure to comply is due to her inability to understand the instruction, Mr. Anastasi will see that she does not respond to certain instructions (e.g., "Get in line"). However, the teacher will also note that she does respond readily to other instructions that she *does* understand, indicating that her motivation to comply with the instructions is good when she is capable of complying.

All children profit from good teaching techniques. Effective teaching techniques have been empirically validated in the literature with children who can be difficult to teach. This technique develops compliance by good teaching of instruction-following skills.

Steps of Guided Practice and Reinforcement

1. Present the instruction once in clear behavioral terms.
2. Provide verbal prompts and gentle guidance (if needed) to demonstrate the specific steps needed for compliance to your instruction or request. *Note.* This may require a written behavioral program and consent of the parents and the IEP team in many states.
3. Provide praise and attention when the child has complied with the request (with your help).
4. Provide less guidance and fewer verbal cues over time as the child begins to show an understanding of the instruction.
5. Use the same procedures for other instructions you present to the child that typically generate errors in compliance.

The instruction or request should be stated in clear terms so that there is no ambiguity as to the behavior expected. After the request is stated, provide verbal prompts, telling the child the specific steps to perform in order to comply. For some children who have limited understanding with respect to teacher directions, it may be necessary to manually guide them through these steps the first few times—in addition to explaining the steps to them—to obtain compliance. Some children need to be shown exactly what is expected of them before they finally get the picture, but once they have it, they do not forget it. This technique may require a written plan submitted to the IEP team and consented to by team members and parents. You should explain to outside reviewers and/or parents that what is being offered with this technique constitutes good teaching and guidance and will not be done in an abrupt and forceful manner.

Once compliance is obtained, praise the child for compliance, even though it occurred with your help. You do not want the child to feel he or she is being pushed to do the task. A child who has received praise will look forward to your help in the future. You can also combine praise and social reinforcement with more tangible incentives and reinforcement such as points, stars, charts, edibles, or free time. After a while, you can begin to provide less guidance and then less explanation as to the specific steps involved in complying to the request as the child demonstrates understanding.

> Mr. Anastasi decides to implement the guided practice and reinforcement strategy based on his hypothesis that Ramona may not understand some part of the instruction to line up. He notes that she sometimes confuses getting in line with other instructions (e.g., "Get in line!" with "Get your lunch!"). Mr. Anastasi begins by stating very clearly (Step 1), "Ramona, it is your turn to line up, behind Barbara." Mr. Anastasi then lightly guides Ramona over to the line (Step 2), in back of Barbara, reiterating the important components of the request ("behind Barbara"). He praises Ramona for her performance (Step 3). "Yes, you are right in line behind Barbara! Very good listening!" He then proceeds to call on the other children, or groups of children. With the second request during the day to line up, Ramona gets right in line behind Barbara. Later that day she is able to get in line behind Tran. Ramona needs help a few times in the next couple of days, but definitely improves in lining up at Mr. Anastasi's request. She now has little problem getting in line when called upon. She has also begun to get her lunch without a problem when requested, indicating that she now understands that instruction as well and does not confuse it with the instruction for getting in line.

The same reservations some teachers raised about using teacher praise are also voiced with respect to guided practice and reinforcement. The two remaining techniques in this booklet also require some additional teacher time initially to learn a new way of dealing with non-compliance. The responses given earlier are appropriate for all the techniques offered in this book. In some cases a teacher may need help on how to best implement the selected strategy with consideration for the other aspects of running a classroom. A behavioral consultant can often design a strategy that both addresses the problem and is sound in terms of other classroom considerations.

Additional Suggestions and Considerations

1. Initially, select just a few instructions or requests with which the child is non-compliant. If the strategy is successful with those initial instructions, you can implement it over a wider range of instructions, tasks, and settings, and with other children.

2. Always provide *enthusiastic* praise for the child's compliance to a request, even when providing additional guidance, especially in the initial phase of implementing this technique. If you do not accompany help and guidance with praise and possibly other tangible rewards, the guidance often becomes aversive to the child.

3. Begin removing the amount of help gradually to ensure that the child learns to comply with the instruction independently.

4. If you are going to award points for compliance (in addition to praise and teacher attention), then draw up a chart that specifies how many points are needed for rewarding items, activities, and events.

5. If the task being requested of the child is lengthy (e.g., consisting of multi-step instructions), consider breaking the task into subtasks and teach one new component at a time.

6. If gentle guidance and other prompts are not effective, you may need to design a specific structured program to teach the child to better understand the instructions. For more information on these techniques, consult the following resources: Cipani (1987, 1991) and Lovaas (1981).

7. If errors begin to occur at any point in the helping process, provide more guidance to the child at that point. Errors are a child's way of telling you that she or he is not sure of what to do.

8. If this technique is successful in dealing with the non-compliance problem, continue its use. If not, try another technique.

Grandma's Rule

In some cases, children are non-compliant because the teacher asks them to do something they do not like, or worse, something they dread. Or, a child may be engaged in a preferred activity such as playing or drawing when asked to begin an activity that is less interesting (such as reading or math seatwork). Additionally, little or no incentive for switching to a less preferred activity is provided. It is easy to see why compliance may be a problem for some children.

> When Susan is asked to run during physical education, she often has to be told many times to begin running. She tries to avoid the activity, not seeking attention from the teacher, and comes up with excuses as to why she cannot run. She is more successful than others in avoiding running. In general, she does not engage in any activities during PE that require her to run or exert herself in some other way without considerable prodding on the part of the teacher. This lends evidence to the possibility that Susan's non-compliance is motivated by her being able to successfully escape and/or avoid these activities a significant percentage of the time combined with the lack of a strong incentive to perform the required tasks.

Recess is the highlight of the school day for most children. Coming back to the class to work on some academic task ranks somewhere below recess for most children (possibly even lower than eating vegetables!). While many children eventually learn this routine and adjust to it, some experience great difficulty when asked to come back into the classroom from a recess period. The teacher may have tried pleading or cajoling, which often does not work or at best is successful only on some occasions. But pleading and cajoling can be tiresome from the standpoint of the teacher and the child, and it quickly loses its power to coerce the child back into the class from recess.

Some teachers feel that ignoring a child's non-compliance to the request "Come inside" will eventually work. While the child may eventually come on any particular day, is ignoring really working? What often results when ignoring is used as a strategy is that although the child eventually comes in, the child has learned to repeatedly ignore the request to come in until she or he is tired of playing and ready to come in. If classrooms or schools were administered with the maxim that all children should decide when to study (and for how long) and when to have recess (and for how long), then ignoring the child who does not come in from recess on time would be a successful strategy!

Grandma was faced with a similar circumstance, for example, getting you to eat your vegetables during dinner when you really disliked them and would rather eat the dessert. She may have seen that, when left to your own devices, you always seemed to develop your stomachache either after eating your dessert or right before you had the "opportunity" to eat your vegetables. Grandma figured that the best way to get you to eat your vegetables was to change the dinner arrangement. You had to finish a small part of your vegetables before you received the dessert. Eating this small amount of vegetables, however environmentally unsound you may have felt their ingestion would be, resulted in your: (a) not having to eat any more vegetables and, (b) getting to eat the dessert. In her own intuitive style, what Grandma did was to use a highly preferred activity such as eating dessert (called a *high probability behavior*) to reinforce your compliance to her request to eat vegetables (called a *lower probability behavior*). Grandma discovered this rule long before behavior analysts, but behavior analysts gave it a name, the *Premack Principle* (Premack, 1959), and took all the credit for uncovering this great principle of human behavior.

How does this example of getting children to eat their vegetables by withholding dessert exemplify a relevant strategy for non-compliant children in the classroom? In the classroom, children demonstrate low levels of compliance to specific teacher requests or tasks they deem to be mildly or moderately aversive. However, there are instructional tasks or noninstructional activities that these children do like. The teacher's task is laid out: Teach the children that when they perform the less preferred instructional task, they get to select a more preferred activity.

Steps to Implementing Grandma's Rule

1. Present the instruction in clear behavioral terms once.

2. State the time limit for complying with the request or instruction.

3. Provide praise and a check on a Compliance Sheet (Figure 1, described below) for each request the child complies with within the allotted time.

4. Do not provide a check for non-compliance.

5. Once the child has received enough checks on the Compliance Sheet, provide access to a highly preferred activity (the child's choice from a menu of possible activities).

6. Also, once the child has received enough checks, cease making requests while the child engages in the preferred activity for the specified period of time (measured with a timer).

State the instruction or request in clear terms so that there is no ambiguity as to the behavior that is expected. The child also needs to be told the time limit for complying with your request. When appropriate, you can indicate your count as the method of determining the length of time to be allotted (e.g., "I'm going to count to five"). In other cases it might be more appropriate to set a timer, such as a portable oven timer or stopwatch (e.g., "I'm setting the timer for 2 minutes. You have 2 minutes to clean up your desk, put your books in your backpack, and get in line").

When the child complies with the request, praise him or her. Social reinforcement should always accompany the provision of other reinforcers. For each occurrence of a targeted compliant behavior, place a check in one of the boxes on the child's Compliance Sheet. The use of a Compliance Sheet allows you to select a certain number of compliant behaviors that have to occur before the child is allowed access to a preferred activity. For example, if the target level of compliant behaviors is three to begin with, then the Compliance Sheet should have three boxes (see Figure 1). This sheet can be placed on the child's desk for easy access or left on a separate table or on a wall chart. When the child receives three checks for compliant behavior, she or he then gets access to a highly preferred activity. The child can select from the reinforcement menu (specified on a behavioral contract) that was previously designed and negotiated with you. (Sample behavioral contracts are available from the author.) Once the student has engaged in the activity(ies) of choice (a timer is set to indicate the end of this free time), you can begin the instructional period again, getting a new Compliance Sheet and placing checks on it for continued compliance. Repeat the same procedure.

If the student does not comply within the time allotted, do not offer any attention or verbal praise, and do not plead for compliance. If the child does not receive a check on the Compliance Sheet, access to the preferred activity will be delayed. If you think the child might need extra help, use the gentle guided practice technique described previously. Once compliant behavior does occur, you can provide reinforcement by praising the child and placing a check on the Compliance Sheet.

You can construct your own Compliance Sheets to be tailored to children's individual needs. It would be wise to develop 8 to 10 prototypes of different sheets (e.g., three-check, four-check, five-check, etc.) to facilitate future use.

FIGURE 1
A Three-Check Compliance Sheet

Session 1

			END

Session 2

			END

Session 3

			END

Session 4

			END

Use the Compliance Sheet you feel would allow the child to achieve success initially (e.g., a three-check sheet). After the child has achieved success with the three-check sheet, you can change to one that requires more checks. As the child gets better at complying with teacher instructions and requests, increase the number of check boxes on the sheet.

Ms. Yamaguchi, the PE teacher, designs a performance-based system for Susan. It requires her to perform four exercises during the PE period ((Steps 1 and 2). Ms. Yamaguchi constructs a four-check Compliance Sheet with four boxes. Each time Susan performs an exercise to the desired level, she praises Susan and marks a check in the box (Step 3) of the Compliance Sheet. If Susan does not perform the exercise, she does not get a check (Step 4). When she has a check in each of the four boxes, she can then choose an alternate activity for 10 minutes (Steps 5 and 6), including resting, from a menu labeled "Time-Off Menu." This menu consists of events and reinforcers developed specifically for her. When her 10 minutes are up, she does two more exercises and checks off two boxes on the new Compliance Sheet given to her. Each time Susan comes to PE she is handed a Compliance Sheet specifying the number of checks she must obtain to earn the access to the Time-Off Menu She is then given a list of physical education tasks she is to perform. After 2 weeks, the PE teacher reports that Susan is complying with her schedule 80% of the time (i.e., performs all tasks assigned and earns time off) and that she is now on a five-check Compliance Sheet. This is a dramatic improvement over her baseline level, where she averaged only one or two exercises performed per PE period.

Ms. Yamaguchi is convinced that Susan would have continued her non-compliance during PE if she had not initiated this plan. Ms. Yamaguchi's colleagues tease her, stating that Susan is "winning" because she only participates in a few activities, but Ms. Yamaguchi states that a few exercises are better than no exercises and that *over time* Susan's amount of exercise will increase. Besides, having a predetermined plan for Susan greatly decreases the amount of time Ms. Yamaguchi spends in cajoling and reprimanding.

Additional Suggestions and Considerations

1. Begin this program by selecting a few instructions or requests. If this strategy is successful with those instructions, you can then implement it over a wider range of instructions, tasks, and settings, and with different people.

2. Initially draw up a behavioral contract between student and teacher (when appropriate) that specifies how checks are earned and what events or objects can be accessed when the row on the Compliance Sheet is filled.

3. Ensure not only that successful completion of instructions or tasks leads to the child's accessing preferred events for a certain amount of time, but also that such time is devoid of additional requests or instructions from you (in other words, give the child a break).

4. Start with a Compliance Sheet that requires a minimal amount of compliance and gradually move to one that requires more checks for time off.

5. Verify the child's compliance to the instructional request or task prior to awarding the check.

6. If this technique is successful in dealing with the non-compliance problem, continue its use. If not, try another technique.

Behavioral Momentum

In some cases, a child has a long history of non-compliance, especially to certain requests or instructions. The child finds these requests from the teacher to be extremely aversive and often engages in severe disruptive and/or tantrum behavior when presented with such requests. Going "toe to toe" with these non-compliant children can often result in tantrums, crying, and whining. In some cases a child may act out verbally and/or physically toward the teacher. Particularly when these other severe behaviors accompany the child's non-compliance, it is wise to attempt to get compliance by modifying the context in which you present the instruction or request.

> The third grade teacher, Ms. Gonzalez, knows that when she asks Bob to take out his math book, he usually whines and resists until either he gives in or Ms. Gonzalez gives up. To avoid having this scenario played out again and again, Ms. Gonzalez decides to try another tactic by first presenting him with simple requests or instructions (i.e., requests that are likely to result in compliance). Ms. Gonzalez feels that if she could just begin on a positive note and obtain compliance to requests that Bob is likely to comply with, then a *momentum of compliance* would be built so that when she "slipped" in the feared request, Bob would be more likely to comply.

There are plenty of examples of situations in which a teacher should rely on building a momentum of compliance to get the child or children to comply with a request that is probably not going to be readily accepted. An everyday example can be found in preschool and kindergarten classes. Some young children have an extremely hard time complying when asked to pick up the toys they were playing with and put them back in the cupboards or baskets. With some children, just mentioning that it is time to clean up is a signal for them to run out of the area, classroom, and/or building. Often, continued requests to pick up the toys result in "selective hearing loss" or worse, crying and tantrums. It becomes aversive for the teacher even to make these requests of such children, so much so that the teacher eventually stops asking them to clean up after themselves.

Wise teachers who quickly identify non-compliant children will realize that they should not request these children to pick up their toys without advance preparation. The wise teacher might go over to such a child and ask a question about the child's play activity (e.g., "What are you doing?"). The teacher might then ask the child to hand him or her one of the toys so they can put it away. When the child complies with this, the teacher praises the child and then asks him or her in a positive tone to put away two or three toys. When the child complies to this request, the teacher offers praise. ("Oh! I love it when you are so thoughtful in putting away your toys.") The next time this child needs to put away the toys, the teacher follows the same sequence, asking the child to put away a greater number of toys. This gradual shaping of the child's compliance to the teacher's request is used on subsequent days until the teacher has the child engaging readily in the desired behavior. The technical term for this approach is *behavioral momentum.*

To understand the behavioral momentum technique (Mace et al., 1988) it is necessary to become familiar with two new terms. Commands that are likely to be followed are called *high-P* (high-probability). Commands that the child does not like are called *low-P* (low-probability) commands. This technique simply involves developing a relationship between these two sets of commands.

Steps of Behavioral Momentum

1. Present three to five high-P commands (time needed to comply with a command no longer than 3 to 5 seconds), and *praise and reward compliance.*

2. Present the low-P command, and *praise and reward compliance.*

3. Failure to obtain compliance to the low-P command should result in providing two to four more high-P commands before re-presenting the low-P command.

4. When the child complies with the low-P command, reinforce compliance by allowing the child access to a preferred object or activity.

5. This strategy is particularly suited for young children, regardless of level of disability. With other older children, substitute positive conversation prior to presenting a low-P command.

In developing a momentum of compliance, present three to five high-P commands that can be complied with in a few seconds (e.g., "Can you touch your nose?", "Can you shake my hand?", "What is your last name?" "What day of the week is it?" "Raise your arms above your head,") (Step 1). The tone for the questions is one of invitation, not confrontation. Socially reinforce the child for complying to these high-P commands. When you feel that the child is complying readily, give the low-P command in a positive, inviting tone (Step 2). Verbally encourage the child to engage in the behavior (e.g., "I'll bet you can do it!"). Heavily reinforce compliance to the low-P command (Step 4). If the child does not comply readily, go back to easier high-P commands, reinforcing compliance, and then present the low-P command again in the manner described above (Step 3), but with a little more guidance and help (see the guided practice technique described earlier). Praise the child heavily for his or her tremendous effort. Be sure not to present another low-P command after obtaining compliance with the initial low-P command. Be happy with small victories in the beginning. Following compliance to the low-P command, allow the child to select one or several preferred activities as a reinforcer.

> Mr. Jones, a first grade teacher, decides to use behavioral momentum as the treatment strategy for Alessandra's noncompliance during oral reading. Mr. Jones feels Alessandra may be hesitant or fearful of reading aloud to the class. Mr. Jones identifies three to five high-P commands for which compliance can be obtained readily from Alessandra. These include giving her name and birthday, the date, and other factual information. Mr. Jones starts by sitting next to Alessandra during oral reading and asking her to say her name, state her birthday, and state what month it is and then reinforcing her for correct responses (Step 1). He then asks Alessandra to read the title aloud (low-P command, Step 2). When Alessandra reads the title, Mr. Jones socially reinforces her, gives her points on her card, and then moves to someone else (Step 2). Note that Alessandra is successful on her first attempt. This is important for the next attempt. Each time Alessandra is asked to read aloud, Ms. Jones provides a few easy questions to "warm her up." He uses varied questions, so it will not look unusual to the other children. Then he asks Alessandra to read increasing numbers of words while she moves farther and farther away. Sometimes he gives her extra time on the computer for completing a passage of oral reading (Step 4). After the second day, Alessandra is reading in front of the group with little hesitation, and Mr. Jones no longer sees the need to provide high-P commands prior to asking her to read a passage in the book.

Additional Suggestions and Considerations

1. Begin this program by selecting a *few* low-P commands to be targeted. If this strategy is successful with these initial commands, you can implement it over a wider range of low-P commands.

2. Reinforce compliance to low-P commands both by praise and by tangible rewards. In the beginning, do not present several low-P commands consecutively. As the child gets better at compliance, the number of low-P commands can be increased.
3. Provide the child with help if you feel this will encourage him or her to get going when you give the low-P command.
4. This program can also contain elements of the other approaches—Grandma's Rule, guided practice, or teacher praise for compliance. Particularly if this strategy is unsuccessful, consider incorporating the other techniques discussed in this manual with behavioral momentum.

Conclusion

To deal with children who are non-compliant, a teacher should have an array of techniques that can be used for individual children. One technique will not be satisfactory for dealing with all non-compliant children you may face during your teaching career. This manual presented four techniques that can be the basis of a set of tools for handling such children. These four techniques do not exhaust the range of techniques available from the research literature, but they have been found effective in dealing with non-compliance.

References

Cipani, E. (1987). Errorless learning technology: Theory, research and practice. In R. P. Barrett & J. L. Matson (Eds.), *Advances in developmental disorders (Vol. 1*, pp. 237–275). Greenwich, CT. JAI.

Cipani, E. (1991). *A guide to developing language competence in preschool children with severe and moderate handicaps.* Springfield, IL: Charles C Thomas.

Litow, L., & Pumroy, D. K. (1975). A brief review of classroom group-oriented contingencies. *Journal of Applied Behavioral Analysis, 8,* 341–347.

Lovaas, O. I. (1981). *Teaching developmentally disabled children: The "Me" book.* Austin, TX: Pro-Ed.

Mace, F. C., Hock, M. L., Lalli, J. S., West, B. J., Belfiore, P., Pinter, E., & Brown, D. K. (1988). Behavioral momentum in the treatment of non-compliance. *Journal of Applied Behavioral Analysis, 21,* 123–141.

Premack, D. (1959). Toward empirical behavioral laws: I. Positive reinforcement. *Psychological Review, 66,* 219–233.

Roberts, M. W., McMahon, R. J., Forehand, R., & Humphreys, L. (1978). The effect of parental instruction-giving on child compliance. *Behavior Therapy, 9,* 793–798.

CEC Policy on Physical Intervention

The Council recognizes the right to the most effective educational strategies to be the basic educational right of each special education child. Furthermore, the Council believes that the least restrictive positive educational strategies should be used, as it relates to physical intervention, to respect the child's dignity and personal privacy. Additionally, the Council believes that such interventions shall assure the child's physical freedom, social interaction, and individual choice. The intervention must not include procedures which cause pain or trauma. Lastly, behavior intervention plans must be specifically described in the child's written educational plan with agreement from the education staff, the parents, and, when appropriate, the child.

The Council recommends that physical intervention be used only if **all** the following requirements are met:

- The child's behavior is dangerous to herself/himself or others, or the behavior is extremely detrimental to or interferes with the education or development of the child.

- Various positive reinforcement techniques have been implemented appropriately and the child has repeatedly failed to respond as documented in the child's records.

- It is evident that withholding physical intervention would significantly impede the child's educational progress as explicitly defined in his/her written educational plan.

Adopted by the CEC Delegate Assembly, 1993
San Antonio, Texas

- The physical intervention plan specifically will describe the intervention to be implemented, the staff to be responsible for the implementation, the process for documentation, the required training of staff, and supervision of staff as it relates to the intervention and when the intervention will be replaced.
- The physical intervention plan will become part of the written educational plan.
- The physical intervention plan shall encompass the following provisions:
    - A comprehensive analysis of the child's environment including variables contributing to the inappropriate behavior;
    - The plan to be developed by a team including professional and parents/guardians, as designated by state/provincial and federal law;
    - The personnel implementing the plan shall receive specific training congruent with the contents of the plan and receive ongoing supervision from individuals who are trained and skilled in the techniques identified in the plan;
    - The techniques identified in the physical intervention plan are approved by a physician to not be medically contraindicated for the child (a statement from the physician is necessary); and
    - The impact of the plan on the child's behavior must be consistently evaluated, the results documented, and the plan modified when indicated.

The Council supports the following prohibitions:

- Any intervention that is designed to, or likely to, cause physical pain;
- Releasing noxious, toxic or otherwise unpleasant sprays, mists, or substances in proximity to the child's face;
- Any intervention which denies adequate sleep, food, water, shelter, bedding, physical comfort, or access to bathroom facilities;
- Any intervention which is designed to subject, used to subject, or likely to subject the individual to verbal abuse, ridicule, or humiliation, or which can be expected to cause excessive emotional trauma;

- Restrictive interventions which employ a device or material or objects that simultaneously immobilize all four extremities, including the procedure known as prone containment, except that prone containment may be used by trained personnel as a limited emergency intervention;
- Locked seclusion, unless under constant surveillance and observation;
- Any intervention that precludes adequate supervision of the child; and
- Any intervention which deprives the individual of one or more of his or her senses.

The Council recognizes that emergency physical intervention may be implemented if the child's behavior poses an imminent and significant threat to his/her physical well-being or to the safety of others. The intervention must be documented and parents/guardians must be notified of the incident.

- However, emergency physical intervention shall not be used as a substitute for systematic behavioral intervention plans that are designed to change, replace, modify, or eliminate a targeted behavior.
- Furthermore, the Council expects school districts and other educational agencies to establish policies and comply with state/provincial and federal law and regulations to ensure the protection of the rights of the child, the parent/guardian, the education staff, and the school and local educational agency when physical intervention is applied.

CEC Mini-Library
Exceptional Children at Risk

A set of 11 books that provide practical strategies and interventions for children at risk.

- *Programming for Aggressive and Violent Students.* Richard L. Simpson, Brenda Smith Miles, Brenda L. Walker, Christina K. Ormsbee, & Joyce Anderson Downing. No. P350. 1991. 42 pages.

- *Abuse and Neglect of Exceptional Children.* Cynthia L. Warger with Stephanna Tewey & Marjorie Megivern. No. P351. 1991. 44 pages.

- *Special Health Care in the School.* Terry Heintz Caldwell, Barbara Sirvis, Ann Witt Todaro, & Debbie S. Accouloumre. No. P352. 1991. 56 pages.

- *Homeless and in Need of Special Education.* L. Juane Heflin & Kathryn Rudy. No. P353. 1991. 46 pages.

- *Hidden Youth: Dropouts from Special Education.* Donald L. MacMillan. No. P354. 1991. 37 pages.

- *Born Substance Exposed, Educationally Vulnerable.* Lisbeth J. Vincent, Marie Kanne Poulsen, Carol K. Cole, Geneva Woodruff, & Dan R. Griffith. No. P355. 1991. 30 pages.

- *Depression and Suicide: Special Education Students at Risk.* Eleanor C. Guetzloe. No. P356. 1991. 45 pages.

- *Language Minority Students with Disabilities.* Leonard M. Baca & Estella Almanza. No. P357. 1991. 56 pages.

- *Alcohol and Other Drugs: Use, Abuse, and Disabilities.* Peter E. Leone. No. P358. 1991. 33 pages.

- *Rural, Exceptional, At Risk.* Doris Helge. No. P359. 1991. 48 pages.

- *Double Jeopardy: Pregnant and Parenting Youth in Special Education.* Lynne Muccigrosso, Marylou Scavarda, Ronda Simpson-Brown, & Barbara E. Thalacker. No. P360. 1991. 44 pages.

Save 10% by ordering the entire library, No. P361, 1991. Call for the most current price information, 703/620-3660.

Send orders to:
The Council for Exceptional Children, Dept. K30950
1920 Association Drive, Reston VA 22091-1589

CEC Mini-Library
Working with Behavioral Disorders

Edited by Lyndal M. Bullock and Robert B. Rutherford, Jr.

A set of nine books developed with the practitioner in mind.

Use this Mini-Library as a reference to help staff understand the problems of specific groups of youngsters with behavioral problems.

- *Teaching Students with Behavioral Disorders: Basic Questions and Answers.* Timothy J. Lewis, Juane Heflin, & Samuel A. DiGangi. No. P337. 1991. 37 pages.

- *Conduct Disorders and Social Maladjustments: Policies, Politics, and Programming.* Frank H. Wood, Christine O. Cheney, Daniel H. Cline, Kristina Sampson, Carl R. Smith, & Eleanor C. Guetzloe. No. P338. 1991. 27 pages.

- *Behaviorally Disordered? Assessment for Identification and Instruction.* Bob Algozzine, Kathy Ruhl, & Roberta Ramsey, No. P339. 1991. 37 pages.

- *Preparing to Integrate Students with Behavioral Disorders.* Robert A. Gable, Virginia K. Laycock, Sharon A. Maroney, & Carl R. Smith. No. P340. 1991. 35 pages

- *Teaching Young Children with Behavioral Disorders.* Mary Kay Zabel. No. P341. 1991. 25 pages.

- *Reducing Undesirable Behaviors.* Edited by Lewis Polsgrove. No. P342. 1991. 33 pages.

- *Social Skills for Students with Autism.* Richard L. Simpson, Brenda Smith Myles, Gary M. Sasso, & Debra M. Kamps. No. P343. 1991. 23 pages.

- *Special Education in Juvenile Corrections.* Peter E. Leone, Robert B. Rutherford, Jr., & C. Michael Nelson. No. P344. 1991. 26 pages.

- *Moving On: Transitions for Youth with Behavioral Disorders.* Michael Bullis & Robert Gaylord-Ross. No. P345. 1991. 52 pages.

Save 10% by ordering the entire library, No. P346, 1991. Call for the most current price information, 703/620-3660.

Send orders to:
The Council for Exceptional Children, Dept. K30950
1920 Association Drive, Reston VA 22091-1589